MOTION IN POETRY

20 Traditional poems

RJ Saxon

RJ Saxon

Table of contents

1.

A Day At The See Side

Looking out the window on a hot sunny day.

A wide smile on my face.

Were going out today.

To a place where my childhood memories were made.

Been a few weeks attempting to muster the courage.

To get myself out and join the Scurrage.

I'm usually at home and rarely go out.

But lately four walls are beginning to shout.

Overwhelming seclusion panics anxiety.

I need to get myself back into society.

I decided last night to take a day trip.

After seeing an ad in a video clip.

Kinda ironic that I seen this ad.

As ten minutes earlier I thought I was mad.

A voice from the wall said.

'You must take a break'

A subliminal thought of a sea or a lake.

I'm off to the beach you see.

And I'm taking my bucket and spade with me.

I've a small bag with lunch.

Just right for a munch.

Think i'll have it round two.

Just in time for late brunch.

I dressed accordingly brown sandals white socks.

And an old pair of flip flops.

To walk by the rocks.

So I'm off and I'm out of this god damn flat.

With my cargo shorts on and a panama hat.

I've never been one to follow the fashion.

Dreams of the seaside is my favorite passion.

I love the feel of the sand in my toes.

But not to keen of other places it goes.

Those scratchy pieces of Aragonite.

Will be working their way down my pants tonight.

But anyway not gonna let that spoil my fun.

I'm out for the day gonna bask in the sun.

Laying out my towel on the hot silky sand.

A stranger walked up with a note in his hand.

I straightened my towel.

Placed my bucket and spade.

And asked the stranger was my post delayed.

The stranger said.

'No, What your'e seeing's not real'

The note your'e holding is augmented just feel.

I looked with confusion at the note that was blank.

My surroundings strange like in a fish tank.

Daylight turned darkness the stranger disappeared.

I removed the headset with frustration and fear.

Back to reality back in the flat.

Maybe one day I'll make my way back.

2.

A Minds Contemplation

Gazing upon a star filled sky.

I ponder it's meaning and question why.

This life we live why was we born.

A mystery to many a tale forlorn.

A ticking clock a time man made.

From day to night our live's our played.

The perpetual rhythm we casually endure.

Never asking if there is more.

In god we trust a popular saying.

A religious belief of a Diety portraying.

Monetary values first.

This evil world is at it's worst.

Your conscience is clear you are the creator.

Never say 'I'll do that later'

Your time is precious do it now.

No more what when where and how's.

This game of life this fun house cycle.

Inside yourself is more Inciteful.

At the end of your purpose and your at your rest.

You can always say you did your best.

3.

At The End Of Love And Life

Each day I miss your warm embrace.

The feel of your hands upon my face.

Your delicate lips.

They connect with mine.

Such a sensual feeling.

It seemed to stop time.

I hide my heartache.

Behind a wrinkled old face.

The occasional tear.

As I sit in this place.

The nurses they're nasty.

Don't help with my ails.

My body aches.

So fragile and frail.

I stare through the window.

Now bound to two wheels.

No one around me.

Knows how I feel.

If only they could see.

How we danced and we laughed.

Portrayed by my bedside.

In an old photograph.

Memories I keep.

So close to my heart.

It pains me inside.

Now that we are apart.

Years of companionship.

Love and trust.

A relationship gone.

Now turned to rust.

The world around me.

Now an empty shell.

As I age ungracefully.

In a heartbreak hell.

Awaiting the day I can meet you again.

And replay our memories, exactly the same.

4.

Bonfire Night

'Penny for the guy' we all would cry.

As we walked through the streets

to earn money we'd try.

Pushing a pram with with a dummy named 'Fawkes'

Made from old clothes a face outlined with chalk.

We spent the whole day lumbering timber.

Watching it burn turning to cinder.

Dragging old doors on our backs to the fire.

Then place on the guy like a mock funeral pyre.

As a child excited when day turned to night.

Watching the fireworks ignite and take flight.

A rocket lifts off it fires so high.

A pop explosion Illuminates the sky.

A whizz and a bang catherine wheel starts to spin.

The children's gloved hands hold their dear next of kin.

A giant sparkler trails light through the air.

As children wave them with confident flair.

Toffee and parkin consumed by the crowds.

As an aerial display paints the sky so proud.

5.

Brains

Walking the dark and desolate streets.

You can hear if they're close with the shuffling of feet.

Moaning and groaning dim witted and slow.

I'll destroy they're brains with my axe or my bow.

Gruesome non humans in search of fresh blood.

Walk the avenues of my neighborhood.

Unsure of how far this disease has spread.

As I deploy my axe to one straight in it's head.

A rotting corpse falls to the floor.

Just one of many I know there are more.

I carry on searching and hope to see.

If there other normal's and it's not just me.

14

A government experiment gone horribly wrong.

An apocalyptic ending the worlds last swan song.

With midnight approaching I walk the route back.

To an empty home supplies in a sack.

This town now searched I have to move on.

Friends and family are dead and gone.

I sit by the fire contemplate my next plan.

Tomorrow I'll leave in the minivan.

As I fall asleep living nightmare to dream.

A horde of one thousand exposed can be seen.

At the top of the street the growlers arrive.

For the last living human no more have survived.

6.

Breakfast Of Champions

Daylight floods.

Through the window pane.

Hot flushes pulse.

Through every vein.

The toxins flood.

From out my skin.

My mind unaware.

Of the state i'm in.

I sluggishly slide.

From my sweat soaked chair.

Head to the fridge.

There's one in there.

My lips are dry.

My head is heavy.

I popped the top.

On another bevvy.

I'm anxious in frenzy.

Til I take a sip.

From that cold brown bottle.

Upon my lip.

Each morning I tend.

To do the same.

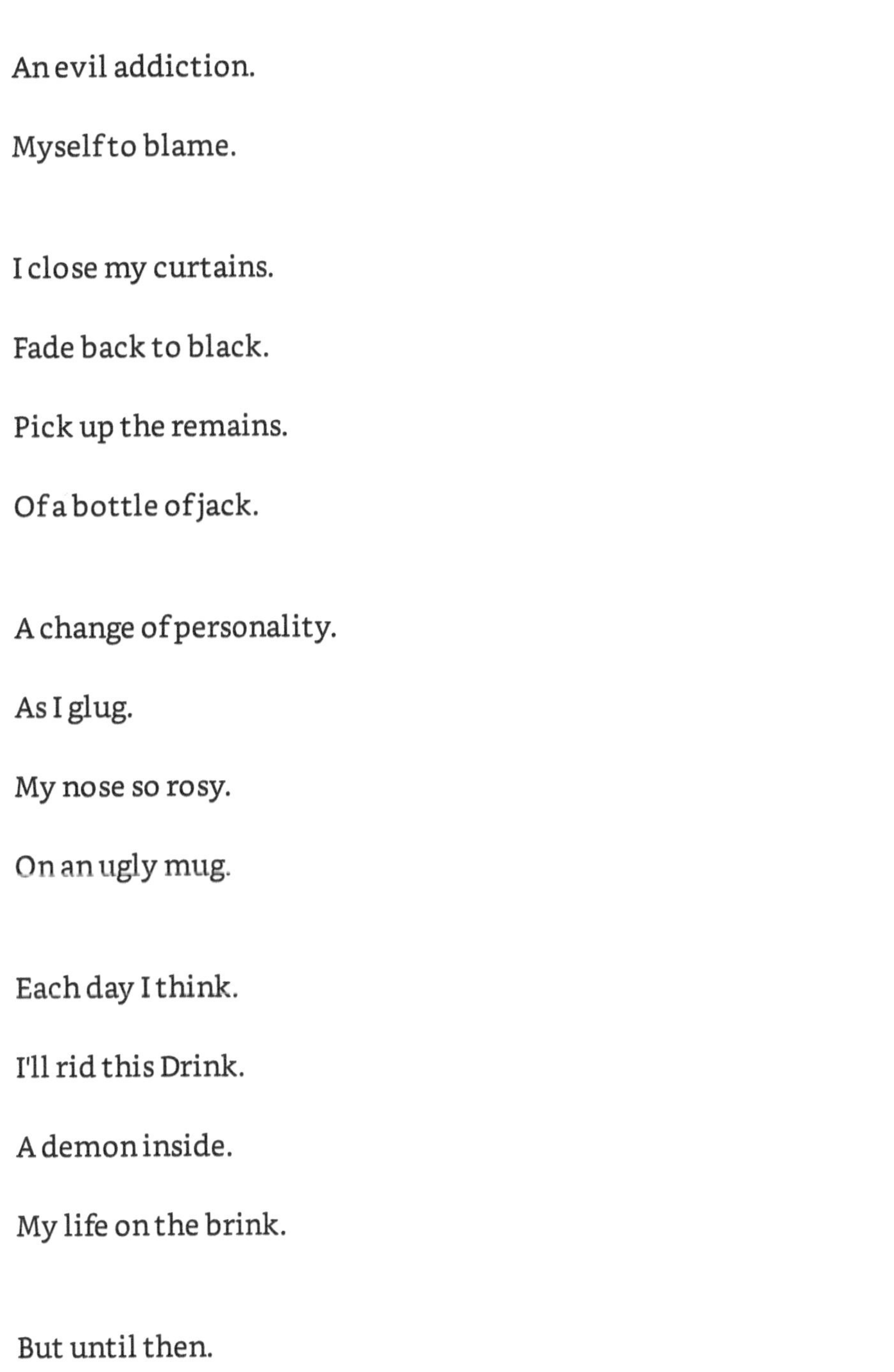

An evil addiction.

Myself to blame.

I close my curtains.

Fade back to black.

Pick up the remains.

Of a bottle of jack.

A change of personality.

As I glug.

My nose so rosy.

On an ugly mug.

Each day I think.

I'll rid this Drink.

A demon inside.

My life on the brink.

But until then.

Let's bring the cheer.

And wash down another

Breakfast beer.

7.

Emotional Disconnection

As I walk through the centre of my hometown.

Peoples faces expressionless no smile nor frown.

Totally oblivious in my path I walk round.

Their minds Engaged solely inside a virtual shroud.

A hand sized piece of metal.

They hold so dear if your not on facebook.

Do not come near.

Thousands of friends inside this matrix cloud.

Their voices so silent but on their social so loud.

Emoji this like follow that.

More annoying videos of peoples domestic cat.

But this is how our world is seen right now.

Through a touch pad screen.

Faces looking down on it.

Avoiding to be seen.

Sometimes it's like I'm on the outside looking in.

Many times tempted to throw my phone in straight in
the bin.

Anger towards this present time all in line like a
bowling pin.

Impossible to rid my own life of this technological sin.

8.

Fairly Fun

Hustle and bustle at the entry gates.

My first adventure at the age of eight.

I was met by a mechanical laughing clown.

It's recorded laugh seemed demonic and loud.

Entombed in a glass box with a harlequin gown.

I walked with my mother through the park to the rides.

Holding my hand tight and close to her side.

I pointed towards the mirrored hall.

My mother said. 'No chance your not that tall'

Passing the arcades and the haunted swing.

A voice from the fun house started to sing.

Enticing any passers by.

To come on in.

Give the fun house a try.

I thought to myself i'll give that a miss.

A friend of mine ended up covered in...

We arrived at my favourite spot.

The smell of donuts all sugary and hot.

Aromas of butter lashed over popcorn.

To the left a stall selling cockles and prawns.

I Checked my height to the weirdest of rides.

More scary than the ghost train right at its side.

I liked it the best.

A magical place.

But a lot of children had tears on their face.

Mad hatters tea parties playing card bridges.

A rabbit a Queen An old Cheshire cat.

'Oh no mum's bought me a kiss me quick hat'

Embarrassed as we walked on through.

To the tunnel of love.

What's a child to do.

A sense of relief as I checked my height.

The attendant said. 'Sorry I'm just not right'

My mum seemed displeased.

Think she wanted to ride it.

I could tell in her face.

As she tried to hide it.

She used to come here with father you see

During her nine months of pregnancy.

My dad had left was now long gone.

He'd left with a woman.

Mum Said 'A wrong one'

The end of the day came quicker than most.

A quick stop in the cafe for tea and toast.

As the roller coaster passed the national post.

It was always the same on the drive back.

The journey seemed quicker after a nap.

My head had melted a bag of rock.

That lay on the back seat next to grandpa's old sock.

Once a month we would come to the fair.

It was quite a long drive for us to get there.

I hope next time I've grown bigger more tall.

So I can get in that god damn mirrored hall.

9.

No Place To Call Home

RJ SAXON

Wrapped up in a woolen blanket.

I shake with cold my bones so old.

So sad of how my life's progressed.

As I pull the blanket to my chest.

I watch as people scurry by.

I hide my emotions try not to cry.

Some people stop to say hello.

Police telling me to go.

Many others are less caring.

Passing by judgmental glaring.

With a plastic cup and a homeless sign.

I beg for change my heart benign.

On a cold harsh and bitter day.

Frosting up my bearded grey.

A wind so sharp against my skin.

I have no home I have no kin.

This is my life this is my pain.

A dirty pavement next to a broken drain.

The daily shoppers now slowly disperse.

As the shops and businesses count their purse.

I count my change from the cup I placed.

It put a small smile upon my face.

For I knew that in the morning.

My bounty would bring some food so warming.

The end of the day had now arrived.

A peaceful night once more deprived.

As darkness falls around me thickly.

I pray to god to take me quickly.

For I have lived a troublesome life.

Filled with sadness confrontational strife.

Everyday I feel so alone.

No friends to talk to.

No mobile phone.

Just an old raggedy beaten up blanket.

A homeless sign.

An old plastic cup.

The clothes on my back.

And an unpublished book.

I toss and I turn through the night with dread.

I pulled cardboard duvet over the top of my head.

The weather not changing.

Still chilled to the bone.

I lay with unrest.

With no place to call home.

10.

Opportunity Knocks

Five years a Teller a job he loathed.

Deposits withdrawals mortgages loans.

He dreamed of a life not shackled but free.

To live out his days more comfortably.

A fortunate day his stars were aligned.

A robber walked in pulled a bag from behind.

He told the Teller.

'Fill it do it quick'

The robber he shouted feeling physically sick.

The Teller fumbled dropped the bag to the floor.

The robber responded his judgement was poor.

A shot was delivered from the masked man at the scene.

The angry assailant fired a bullet clean.

Extreme pain clutching the top of his arm.

A shout from the robber said he'd do me more harm.

'If you don't move your hands from that silent alarm'

The Teller acknowledged filled the bag to the top.

From all five drawers each Teller in shock.

The robber ran quickly through the door that he came.

But little did he know he'd be leaving in shame.

For the bag the Teller dropped it's color and make.

Was exactly like the one he took to the lake.

Under his desk he deftly switched an identical bag.

Full of old bread and bits.

The needle on the dial hovered over empty.

The passenger seat filled with cash of plenty.

First day on the road a month had passed.

Bullet wound in his shoulder a real pain in the..

Turning into a station an attendant appeared.

A clunk from the pump inserted the rear.

He smiled nodded alighted the car.

Headed to the restroom it wasn't that far.

Looking into the mirror to a face quite bereft.

He splashed some water placed his specs to the left
A bag full of cash that was stolen quite sudden.

From a robber with a scream mask and a top with a hood on.

Inside the bag were bundles of hundreds.

Convincingly fooling the masked man he pondered.

A chance encounter with a bank robber he'd plundered.

He adjusted his cap headed back to the car.

Paid the attendant who told him.

'I hope you get far'

Thinking nothing of it the Teller drove on.

checked the bag at his side and leaned back for the ride.

The attendant smiled as the Teller drove off.

He removed some oil from his face with a cloth.

A month watching the Teller had finally paid.

Another bag switch in the passenger that he laid.

Exactly the way the robber was played.

See he knew his movements in his every day life.

His brother had told him then the judge gave him life.

11.

Rekindled

I lie and stare unaware of my surroundings.

A blip on a machine could hear lightly sounding.

Unable to move don't wanna feel like this,

an empty shell consumed with paralysis.

My eyes stare fixed, bright ceiling above,

my mind devoid of feelings of love.

Where was I, what had gone wrong.

Is this the end, my last swan song.

I wont give in I'm gonna keep trying,

mind focused on movement to stop me from dying.

I attempt to move my fingers and thumb,

I have no sensation, feel completely numb.

This feeling was similar when active and healthy,

Distanced from siblings our troubles were plenty.

Loved ones sit by me, they hope and they pray,

That maybe i'll wake resurface one day.

There's so many more things unsaid left to say.

It's all up to me now, whether I go or I stay.

12.

Sleight Of Hand

A majestic audience sit silent in awe.

The magician's trickery had fooled them once more.

A night of true magic the posters did say.

Just half a shilling to watch his display.

A gas lit stage housed an array of deceptions.

But guaranteed to amaze and thrill no exceptions.

The time had come for his final illusion.

Much more intense than the card trick confusion.

The magician wrapped tight in a white straight jacket.

padlock and chains a minute to crack it.

He hung from a rope above a tank filled with water.

Flames burning through with no time to faulter.

He'd done this trick many times before.

But this time the key slipped from his mouth to the

floor.

Too late to signal to his stage hand to the rear.

The audience's face's filled with fear.

The rope burned through he fell in the drink.

Twisting and turning with no time to think.

His panic and struggle seemed part of the play.

But this final trick would take him today.

13.

Spelling 101 With 'Miss Take'

Wiv a run and a dash, am late four me Klass,

Room 101, this spellins no fun,

I no all eye need too spel an to reed.

But my Teecher thinks am so dum.

Terned the handel to the door.

An dropped me book to the floor.

Miss take terns to face me.

She sed.

'Sit down quick, your making me sick.

this lateness will have to cease.'

The rest ov the klass jus gigguled

and laffed as i sat at the table far bak.

From eh to zee the teecher pro seeded

to point a stik at a bord.

'The leters are jum bulled'

I quietly mum bulled.

Miss take aksed me wat did i sey.

I told her 'The leters lucked all bak to frunt'

Sum Jock at the back called me a C***

The bell rang for the end of the klass.

The jock at the bak slapped a girl on the ass.

I cowerd as he walked by me.

The rest of the stewdents.

Left the room with such prudence.

I made my way with enveloped bemusement.

I hed to the next lessun

More wurds more stressin.

See my learnins a mishun wiv my dislecsic condishun.

14.

The Horseman On Old Hallows

Silhouetted figures walk through the night.

Children in costumes they cause such a fright.

It's the time of year when we shout 'Trick or Treat'

Kids knocking the doors on Old Hallows street.

Aptly named from it's frightening history.

A Headless Horseman caused such a mystery.

Thirty first of October his presence in force.

To dash from the woods on a spiritual horse.

Parents carve pumpkins with devilish grins.

To hang in the doorways lit candles within.

Candy apple aroma envelopes the street.

Kids they wait patient for the horseman to see.

Cobwebs in windows a passing black cat.

Long pointed noses an old witches hat.

Macabre celebrations it comes once a year.

Painted faces that fill you with fear.

The time had arrived a Quarter to ten.

Time for the horseman to show up again.

The end of the street facing the woods.

The children watched eager wrapped up coat with hood.

A ghostly shriek from his horse was a sign.

That the horseman was now arriving on time.

The children stood firm on the pavement in file.

As the horseman approached with a stench that was vile.

But this time was different from the usual myth.

Where the horseman rode by then vanished in mist.

This time he reached drew a Hessian sword.

And lopped off the heads of the children in awe.

15.

The Pugilist

Ducking and weaving last round now in sight.

The bell for the twelfth to finish the fight.

To be the victor be the best on this earth.

Giving all to prove his worth.

To be the Champ fulfill his dream.

Let everyone know he's the best on the scene.

Battered and bruised from a series of blows.

His opponent is worse his loss now he knows.

Underestimation of this fighters skill.

His style his grace his overwhelming will.

The Boxer swings leather left and right.

Opponent looks feared at his strength and his might.

A tentative crowd watch with bated breath.

A feint here a feint there then a counter in check.

He's down on the canvas blood pours from his eye.

It's time for this boxer to say goodbye.

An exchange of belts from one to the other.

A sportsman's handshake respect like a brother.

A new champ is born he's better than the rest.

But that's just the start of a fighter's test.

16.

The Smartest Mice

Friday night as I sit in my house.

Patiently waiting to catch that mouse.

Inside the walls each night it scurries.

It don't bother me but my girlfriend worries.

See there's a hole from where the mouse comes and goes.

It's been stealing my cheese nibbling holes in my clothes.

Lately it's been driving me mad took the last of the cheese.

There's no more to be had.

I've no idea how it opened the cooler.

There's a lock on the side It's very peculiar.

If I don't catch it soon.

She said she would leave me.

I'll have it tonight ain't gonna deceive me.

The night arrived the girlfriend's not here.

I set some traps to see if it nears.

Two crumbs of cheese left at the bottom of the cooler.

I'll place it on the traps and try to fool ya.

It's okay if it that plan flaws.

I have a plan B there's a gun in my draw.

A glock 23.

And if that doesn't stop it.

I don't know what will.

This pesky damn mouse.

It's making me ill.

Patiently waiting to catch the mouse.

It comes and goes from a wall in my house.

Midnight arrived.

It's time for the mouse.
To come and steal cheese from my house.

All of a sudden the mouse appeared.
It popped from the hole.
Swag bag to the rear.

Wearing a bandits mask.
And burglars attire.
It signaled up to a mouse.
Considerably higher.

A small piece of rope.
Dangled down from the ceiling.
Over the hole where the mouse was revealing.

This could'nt be true.
What was I to do.
A mouse with a mask on.
And now there were two.

What am I seeing.
Do my eyes deceive me.
If I told my girlfriend.

She'd never believe me.

.

'What is this sorcery' I did shout.
Another pesky rodent helping him out.

Over the traps he deftly swung.
His friend right behind him.
Holding the rungs.
Of a small pair of ladders.
They did dash.
Straight to the cooler.
To steal their stash.

I watched in amazement.
One mouse held the ladders.
The other climbed up.
To the lock with some spanners.

Turning the nuts on the hinge.
That was tight.
It opened the cooler.
No cheese was in sight.

I laughed to myself.

Only eggs that were boiled.

No cheese in the cooler.

Their plan was so foiled.

I carried on laughing.

As they made their way back.

No stash in the swag bag.

No cheese to be had.

Too quick too wise.

To be captured by man.

What was I to do.

But to draw up a plan.

An offer for friendship.

With the smartest mice clan.

I'm not one for killing.

So I made them an offer.

A delivery of cheese.

Just my girlfriend don't bother.

I knew this would go on every night.

Scaring my girlfriend it caused such a fright.

Deciding no more to put up a fight.

I wrote them a letter.

An agreement with rights.

Saturday through Tuesday.

You are not to be seen.

Remember these days.

Do not cause a scene.

These smart little rodents.

Agreed with no fuss.

'As long as the cheese is brought to us'

At last an agreement was set in place.

During these days they should not show their face.

Saturday arrived and I was happy as can be.

My girlfriend arrived at a quarter to three.

But this time she was not alone.

She said she was bringing a gift on the phone.

My girlfriend opened the door with her key.

And said.

'Look what I've bought for thee'

I looked at my girlfriend.

Said 'What's that.'

As she took off her coat and fedora hat.

'Isn't she adorable.'

She proudly did chat.

'I bought from a woman.

On the market named pat.'

'It's a cute little feline.'

'A Siamese cat.

17.

Train Of Thought

Patiently waiting at the old railway station.

The train was running late.

On platform nine the weather was fine.

Still waiting for my mate.

The info sign above my head.

Said. 'Arriving at twenty to two'

I've been here an hour and half now.

Bored with nothing to do.

I decided to count the passengers.

Coming to and from the trains.

It was worse than counting sheep though.

Really racking up my brain.

I took some change from the pocket of my jeans.

To buy a plastic cheese sandwich.

From a dusty old vending machine.

The ones with a financial advantage.

Sliding the coins in one by one.

I wait til it counts my cash.

I pumped in the letters on the pad.

Crossed my fingers.

Hoped not to be had.

See I've been in this situation before.

Ripped off by these mechanical fiends.

It was a coffee dispensing overpriced thing.

Which didn't deliver the cream.

Curly metal wire in the machine started to turn.

The sandwich was nearing the edge now.

My Stomach it started to churn.

Low and behold the package got stuck.

On the edge of the tipping point.

I banged hard on the glass.

Trying to loosen it's grasp.

But it didn't move a muscle.

So with anger and frustration.

At the machine in the station.

I shook it from side to side.

It wasn't the smartest thing to do.

As this beast it started to slide.

from it's thin metal base.

Just missing my face.

The vendor smashed to the floor.

An array of sandwiches came pouring out.

I grabbed mine and made a quick dash.

Commuters swooped around the machine.

Which had spilled an array of it's cash.

Heading quickly down the platform.

Towards the arriving train.

The one with my mate on.

The terribly late one.

To realize I was waiting in vain.

18.

Uncharted Path

Weary and tired with this old daily slog.

Wrestling with life like an old bull frog.

With an aim and a purpose a goal that's in sight.

I'll weather this storm put up a grand fight.

See We are all in a world that's devoid of emotion.

Consumed by the media a subliminal potion.

Buy this buy that eat this drink that.

Think i'll pop a like on that you tube cat.

That's just things that grind up my gears.

I've been bitter and twisted like this for years.

A strange way of thinking some might say.

But were all unique in a similar kind of way.

But i'll keep plodding on in my own little bubble.

Stick to my guns I aint causing no trouble.

Life's about the journey not destination they say.
So i'll Keep travelling on til my dying day.

19.

One For Sorrow

One for sorrow
Two for joy
A popular rhyme
I heard as a boy

From unlucky black cats
To new shoes on a table
Superstition and myth
Tales and fables

The best of years
No worries no stress
But a wrong turn in life
Could end up a mess

But them thoughts evade you

Safe with family that made you
So cherish your youth
Til you're long in the tooth

20.

Myth Of The Hairy Man

He'd waited all night
The beast now in sight
In a wet misty wood
Dew dripped from his hood

The rifle he aimed
At this creature so strange
It sluggishly strolled
Hair matted and old

In a wet misty wood
The beast smelled his blood
The townsfolk they begged him

Rid the beast from the wood

But the beast not alone
Behind him it groaned
The stories said one
Not a mother and son

A second too late
As the mother saw the fate
Of her son hit the floor
A family no more
His father had gone
Same fate with the gun

This story lives on
A mystery foregone
Of what ever happened
To the rifleman
And the fable to the
Myth of the hairy man.

BOOKS BY THIS AUTHOR

The Wonky Zoo

Once upon a time in a world where only animals existed lived a nasty old owl who controlled all other types of animals, in a town called animal town, this town housed perfect animals and had a daily normal routine, until one day animals that had been separated because they were different from animals in animal town decided enough was enough and they devised a plan to break free from their prison and change the separation laws and be free to walk amongst the normal animals.

Thirteen

A collection of 13 science-fiction, horror, humor, and mysterious short stories.